FIRST
DINOSAUR
PICTURE ATLAS

Written by David Burnie

Illustrated by Anthony Lewis

KINGFISHER

LONDON & NEW YORK

Copyright © Macmillan Publishers International Ltd 2007, 2019
This edition published in 2019 by Kingfisher
120 Broadway, New York, NY 10271
Kingfisher is an imprint of Macmillan Children's Books, London
All rights reserved.

Distributed in the U.S. and Canada by Macmillan,
120 Broadway, New York, NY 10271

Library of Congress Cataloging-in-Publication data

Burnie, David.
First dinosaur picture atlas / David Burnie.—1st ed.
p. cm.
Includes index.
1. Dinosaurs—Juvenile literature. 2. Dinosaurs—
Geographical distribution—Juvenile literature. 3. Dinosaurs—
Maps—Juvenile literature. I. Title.
QE861.5.B875 2008
567.9—dc22 2007031019

ISBN: 978-0-7534-7536-2

Illustrations by Antony Lewis
Cover Design by Laura Hall

Kingfisher books are available for special promotions and
premiums. For details contact: Special Markets Department,
Macmillan, 120 Broadway, New York, NY 10271

For more information please visit
www.kingfisherbooks.com

Printed in Malaysia
9 8 7 6 5 4 3 2 1
1TR/1119/WKT/UG/128MA

KEY

country border

state border

disputed border

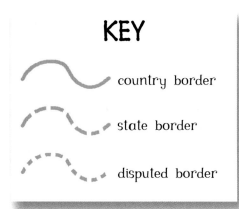

CONTENTS

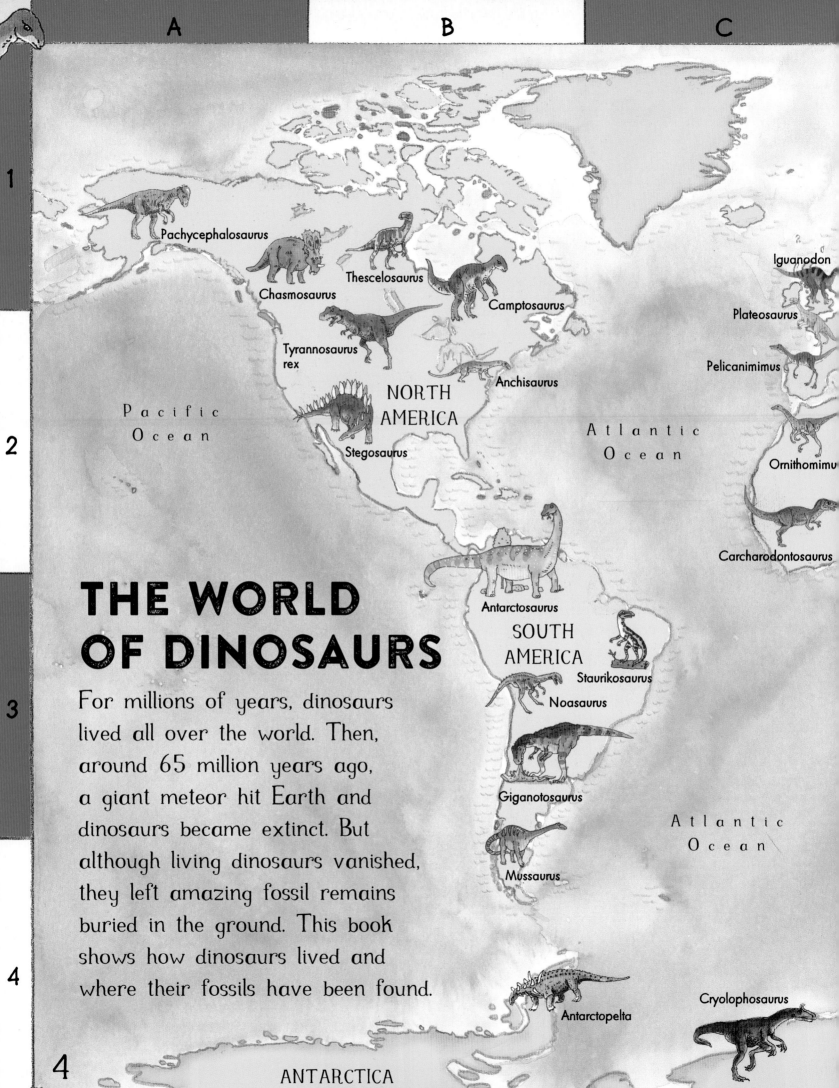

Pachycephalosaurus

Chasmosaurus

Thescelosaurus

Camptosaurus

Tyrannosaurus rex

Anchisaurus

NORTH AMERICA

Pacific Ocean

Stegosaurus

Atlantic Ocean

Iguanodon

Plateosaurus

Pelicanimimus

Ornithomimu

Carcharodontosaurus

Antarctosaurus

SOUTH AMERICA

Staurikosaurus

Noasaurus

Giganotosaurus

Atlantic Ocean

Mussaurus

THE WORLD OF DINOSAURS

For millions of years, dinosaurs lived all over the world. Then, around 65 million years ago, a giant meteor hit Earth and dinosaurs became extinct. But although living dinosaurs vanished, they left amazing fossil remains buried in the ground. This book shows how dinosaurs lived and where their fossils have been found.

Antarctopelta

Cryolophosaurus

ANTARCTICA

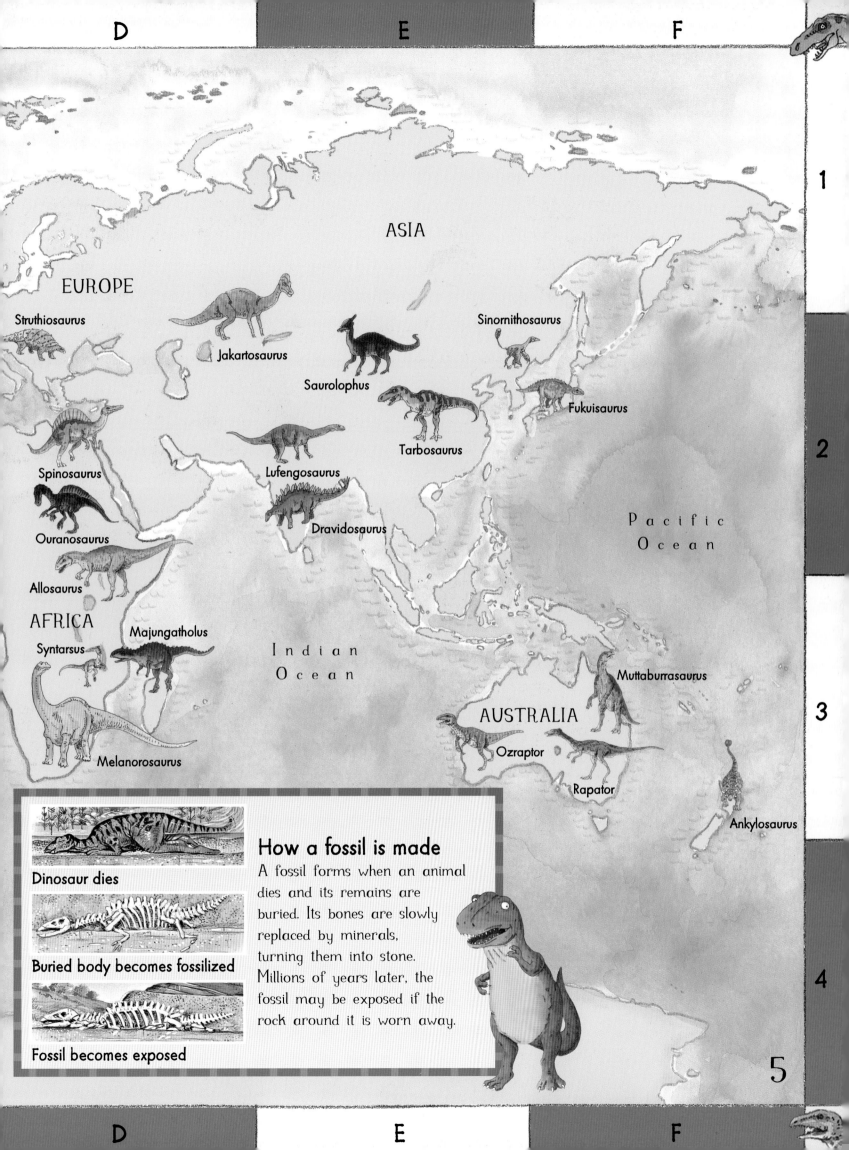

ASIA

EUROPE

Struthiosaurus

Jakartosaurus

Saurolophus

Sinornithosaurus

Fukuisaurus

Tarbosaurus

Spinosaurus

Lufengosaurus

Ouranosaurus

Dravidosaurus

P a c i f i c
O c e a n

Allosaurus

AFRICA

Majungatholus

Syntarsus

I n d i a n
O c e a n

Muttaburrasaurus

AUSTRALIA

Melanorosaurus

Ozraptor

Rapator

Ankylosaurus

How a fossil is made

Dinosaur dies

Buried body becomes fossilized

Fossil becomes exposed

A fossil forms when an animal
dies and its remains are
buried. Its bones are slowly
replaced by minerals,
turning them into stone.
Millions of years later, the
fossil may be exposed if the
rock around it is worn away.

THE AGE OF DINOSAURS

Dinosaurs lived on Earth for more than 160 million years. Scientists split this time into three periods: Triassic, Jurassic, and Cretaceous. During each period, many different dinosaurs evolved and died out. Earth's surface also changed as the continents slowly drifted apart into the seven continents that exist today.

Earth in the Cretaceous period

Compsognathus

Triassic

This period started 251 million years ago. At the beginning of the Triassic, most of the world's land was joined in a huge supercontinent called Pangaea.

Dinosaur hunters

The first dinosaur fossils were dug up in Europe in the 1800s. Since then, dinosaur hunters have found fossils on every continent, including Antarctica. The giant fossilized bones being uncovered here in Niger, Africa, are those of a large plant eater.

Brachiosaurus

Tyrannosaurus rex

Jurassic

This period started around 200 million years ago. In Jurassic times, Pangaea began to break apart. The continents drifted away from one another, taking the animals with them.

Cretaceous

This period began 145 million years ago. It ended 65 million years ago when a huge meteor struck Earth, wiping out the dinosaurs.

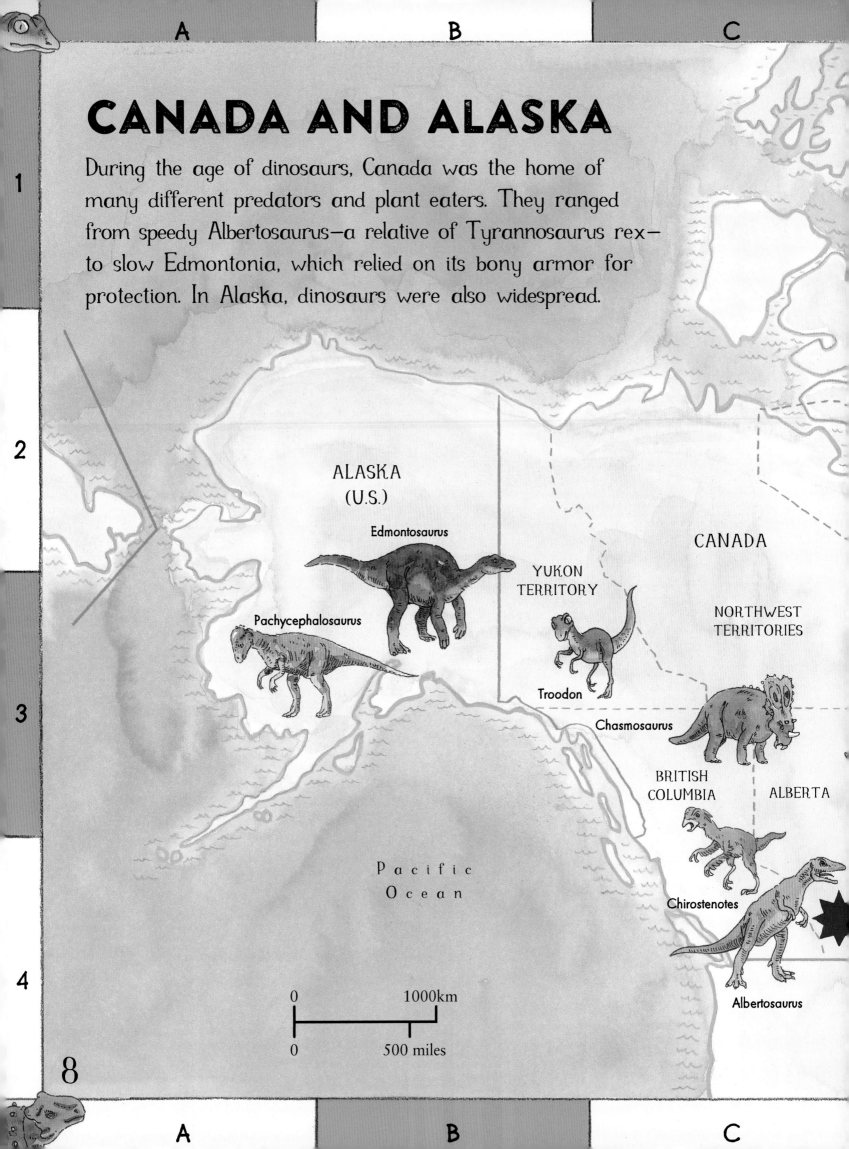

CANADA AND ALASKA

During the age of dinosaurs, Canada was the home of many different predators and plant eaters. They ranged from speedy Albertosaurus—a relative of Tyrannosaurus rex— to slow Edmontonia, which relied on its bony armor for protection. In Alaska, dinosaurs were also widespread.

ALASKA
(U.S.)

Edmontosaurus

Pachycephalosaurus

YUKON
TERRITORY

CANADA

NORTHWEST
TERRITORIES

Troodon

Chasmosaurus

BRITISH
COLUMBIA

ALBERTA

Chirostenotes

Pacific
Ocean

Albertosaurus

0   1000km

0   500 miles

A   B   C

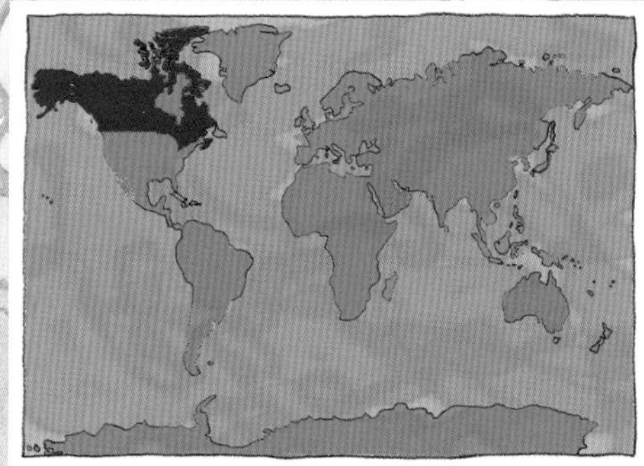

Dinosaur Park

Canada has one of the world's most famous dinosaur graveyards—Dinosaur Provincial Park in southern Alberta. There, almost 40 types of dinosaurs have been found, dating back more than 75 million years.

Look for the star

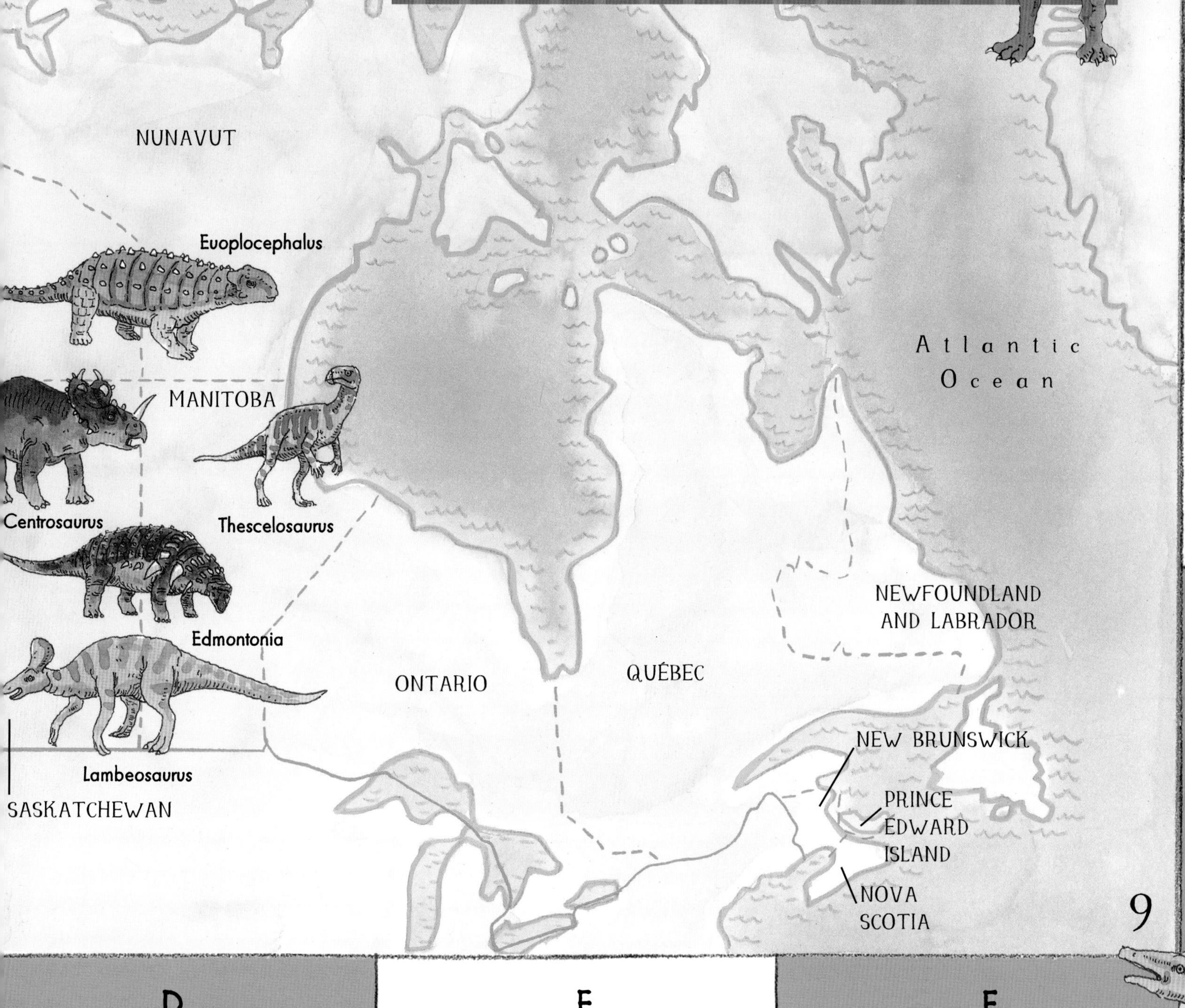

NUNAVUT

Euoplocephalus

MANITOBA

Centrosaurus

Thescelosaurus

Edmontonia

Atlantic Ocean

NEWFOUNDLAND AND LABRADOR

QUÉBEC

ONTARIO

Lambeosaurus

SASKATCHEWAN

NEW BRUNSWICK

PRINCE EDWARD ISLAND

NOVA SCOTIA

PACK ATTACK

In the age of dinosaurs, Canada was a much warmer place than it is today. It was covered by lush plants—making it a perfect feeding ground for Lambeosaurus, a duck-billed dinosaur with a large hollow crest on its head. Lambeosaurus had many enemies, including Dromaeosaurus, which hunted and attacked in groups.

Toothless wonder

Chirostenotes had a bony crest on its head and beak-shaped jaws without any teeth. It hunted smaller animals, pecking at them just like today's birds.

Lambeosaurus

Dromaeosaurus

Just for show

Chasmosaurus had a giant frill behind its head. Instead of being solid, the frill had a bony framework covered with skin. It might have been used to frighten off rivals or attract mates.

Night shift

Troodon had unusually large eyes, which may have helped it hunt at night. It probably chased small mammals that came out to feed when other dinosaurs were asleep.

11

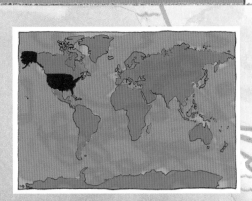

0   1000km

0   500 miles

WASHINGTON

Struthiomimus

Deinonychus

Bambiraptor

 OREGON   Triceratops   Tyrannosaurus rex   MONTANA

Scutellosaurus   Ornitholestes
                                                  WYOMING

Pacific
Ocean   IDAHO

Parasaurolophus   UTAH   Camptosaurus

Diplodocus   COLORADO
            NEVADA
                        Gastonia

                                                  Allosaurus

CALIFORNIA   NEW
                                                  MEXICO

                                    Dilophosaurus
Stegosaurus   ARIZONA

            Coelophysis

                        Scutellosaurus

                                    Seismosaurus

THE UNITED STATES OF AMERICA

The U.S.'s first complete dinosaur—a Hadrosaurus—was discovered in New Jersey in 1858. But most dinosaurs have been found farther west. Dinosaur hunters have unearthed more than 120 types of dinosaurs, from giant plant eaters such as Diplodocus to Tyrannosaurus rex—probably the most famous dinosaur in the world.

Bone bed

The "dinosaur wall" at Dinosaur National Monument in Utah contains hundreds of dinosaur fossils on a ledge of sloping rock. This man is clearing rock, leaving the bones as they were found.

Look for the star

NORTH DAKOTA

Maiasaura

SOUTH DAKOTA

NEBRASKA

MINNESOTA

IOWA

Ceratosaurus

KANSAS

MISSOURI

OKLAHOMA   ARKANSAS

Apatosaurus

TEXAS

Stegoceras

LOUISIANA

WISCONSIN

ILLINOIS

MICHIGAN

INDIANA

OHIO

KENTUCKY

TENNESSEE

MISSISSIPPI

ALABAMA   GEORGIA

FLORIDA

Coelophysis

PENNSYLVANIA

WEST VIRGINIA

VIRGINIA

NORTH CAROLINA

SOUTH CAROLINA

MAINE

VERMONT

NEW HAMPSHIRE

NEW YORK

MASSACHUSETTS

RHODE ISLAND

Anchisaurus

CONNECTICUT

NEW JERSEY

Hadrosaurus   DELAWARE

MARYLAND

Atlantic Ocean

Gulf of Mexico

13

DINOSAUR NEST IN MONTANA

In the 1970s, dinosaur hunters made an incredible find in the mountains of Montana. As well as many fossilized dinosaur bones, they found nests, eggs, and baby dinosaurs. The nests belonged to Maiasaura, or "good mother lizard." This plant-eating dinosaur laid up to 40 eggs in a mound-shaped nest and brought food to its young.

Maiasaura

Protoceratops fossilized eggs

Dinosaur eggs

Like reptiles today, most dinosaurs laid eggs. Compared to their size, dinosaur eggs were often quite small. Some were round, and others were long and narrow. These eggs were laid by Protoceratops, a dinosaur that lived in Mongolia (north-central Asia).

Growing up

When newly hatched, Maiasaura had a tiny skull and teeth that were smaller than a two-year-old child's. As it grew, its skull became bigger and longer, giving it a strong bite for crushing plants.

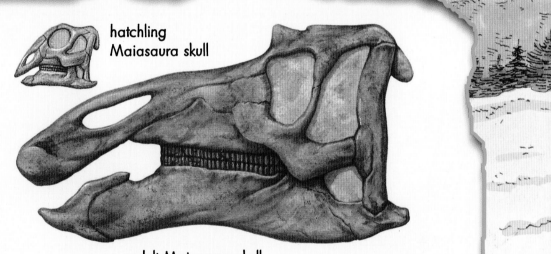

hatchling Maiasaura skull

adult Maiasaura skull

NORTH AMERICAN DINOSAURS

Triceratops looked fierce, but it was actually a plant eater. It was up to four times as heavy as a rhinoceros, and its horns could be as much as three feet (one meter) long. It used its horns to fight strong predators such as Tyrannosaurus rex.

Tyrannosaurus rex

Triceratops

King of the dinosaurs

Tyrannosaurus rex was one of the biggest two-legged predators, and it lived at the end of the age of dinosaurs. It ambushed smaller dinosaurs, but it also scavenged on the dead remains of other dinosaurs.

Tyrannosaurus rex

Scutellosaurus

Danger in numbers

Slim, lightweight, and fast-moving, Deinonychus hunted in a pack. This dinosaur was able to catch and kill larger dinosaurs that moved too slowly to escape.

Tenontosaurus

Deinonychus

Deadly swing

Ankylosaurus had armored skin and a tail club that weighed up to 110 pounds (45 kilograms). By swinging its club, it could smash open the skull of a large predator.

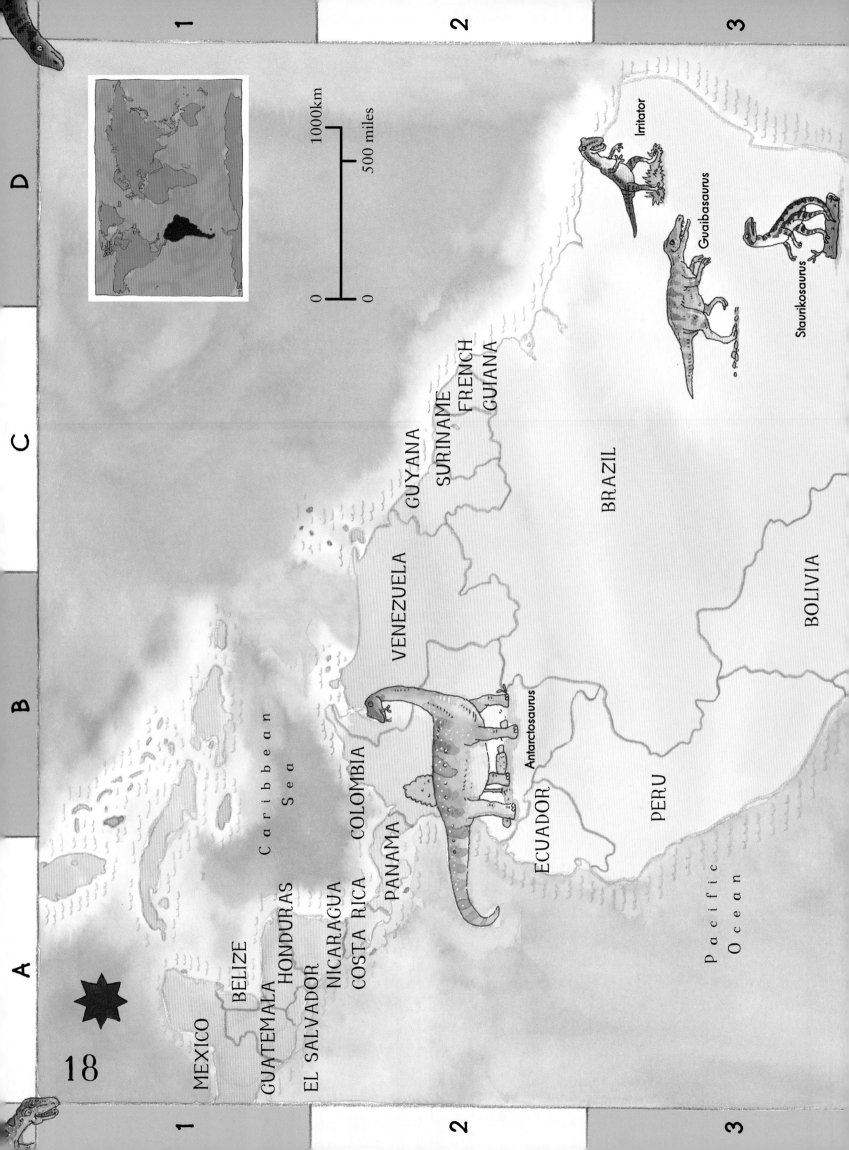

1

2

3

A

B

C

D

MEXICO

BELIZE

GUATEMALA

HONDURAS

EL SALVADOR

NICARAGUA

COSTA RICA

PANAMA

COLOMBIA

VENEZUELA

GUYANA

SURINAME

FRENCH GUIANA

ECUADOR

BRAZIL

PERU

BOLIVIA

Antarctosaurus

Caribbean Sea

Pacific Ocean

1000km

500 miles

0

0

Irritator

Guaibasaurus

Staurikosaurus

CENTRAL AND SOUTH AMERICA

Some of the world's earliest and biggest dinosaurs have been discovered in South America. These include Eoraptor, a chicken-size dinosaur that lived more than 225 million years ago, and Saltasaurus, a colossal plant eater that may have weighed almost 100 tons.

PARAGUAY

ARGENTINA

URUGUAY

Saltasaurus

Herrerasaurus

Noasaurus

Giganotosaurus

Eoraptor

Carnotaurus

Argentinosaurus

Abelisaurus

Piatnitzkysaurus

Mussaurus

CHILE

The crater is under the sea

Experts think that dinosaurs died out after a giant meteor crashed into Earth 65 million years ago. A huge crater has been found in the sea off the coast of Mexico, showing where the meteor might have struck.

Look for the star

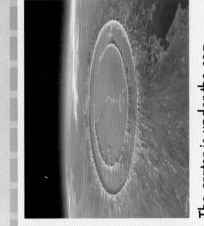

4 5 6

A B C D

DINOSAUR HUNTERS IN ARGENTINA

In Argentina's Valley of the Moon, scientists have found fossils of some of the earliest dinosaurs. One of them, Herrerasaurus, lived 228 million years ago. It was 20 feet (6 meters) long and hunted by running on its back legs.

fossilized skeleton of a Piatnitzkysaurus

Out of reach

Like many hunting dinosaurs, Piatnitzkysaurus had huge back legs but tiny arms. It also had only three fingers on each of its hands.

Handy work

Eoraptor is another very early dinosaur that lived in the Valley of the Moon. Small and quick, it probably ate small animals as well as plants. It could hold the food it caught in its five-fingered hands.

Going to extremes

Giganotosaurus lived more than 100 million years after Herrerasaurus and Eoraptor. It was one of the biggest hunting dinosaurs, weighing as much as seven tons.

Herrerasaurus

Eoraptor

SOUTH AMERICAN DINOSAURS

Carnotaurus was one of the strangest dinosaurs from South America. Its skin was covered with knobby scales, and it had a small head, with a horn above each eye. It might have used the horns like bulls do when they fight rivals to win the right to mate with a female. The name Carnotaurus means "meat-eating bull."

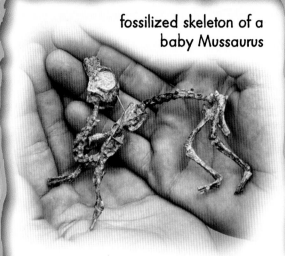

fossilized skeleton of a baby Mussaurus

Tiny dino

The smallest complete dinosaur fossil is a baby Mussaurus from Argentina. It measures only seven inches long. Mussaurus fed on plants. When fully grown, it probably grew to 16 feet (5 meters).

Carnotaurus

Tipping the scales

Saltasaurus was a plant eater that lived in Argentina. Its back was covered with hard bony plates, like those that protect today's crocodiles.

Slashing claw

Noasaurus might have had slashing claws on its hands. Measuring only 8 feet (2½ meters) from head to tail, it would have been light enough to be able to leap on its prey.

EUROPE

In Europe, dinosaur fossils have been studied since the early 1800s, when naturalists figured out that they belonged to giant extinct reptiles. Since then, a huge variety of fossils have been found, including giant plant eaters such as Brachiosaurus and also Baryonyx—one of the few dinosaurs that ate mostly fish.

Early bird

Europe's fossils include many other prehistoric animals besides dinosaurs. The world's earliest known bird, called Archaeopteryx, was discovered in a limestone quarry in southern Germany. Around the size of a crow, it had teeth and a long, bony tail. However, it also had feathers and could fly.

Can you find Archaeopteryx?

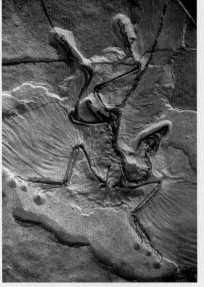

fossilized skeleton of an Archaeopteryx

North Sea

SCOTLAND

Saltasaurus

UNITED KINGDOM

Megalosaurus

NORTHERN IRELAND

Eustreptospondylus

WALES

ENGLAND

IRELAND

NETHERLANDS

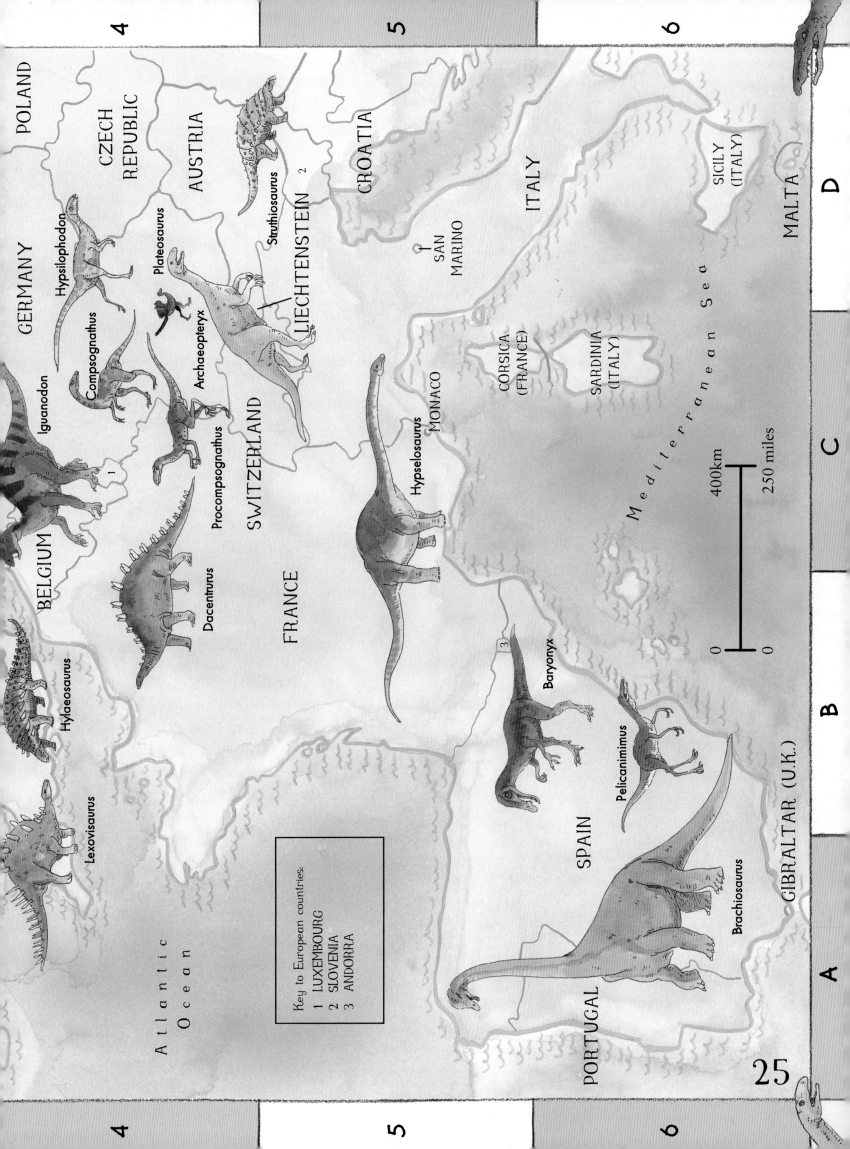

POLAND

CZECH REPUBLIC

AUSTRIA

Struthiosaurus

LIECHTENSTEIN 2

CROATIA

ITALY

SAN MARINO

SICILY (ITALY)

MALTA

GERMANY

Hypsilophodon

Compsognathus

Plateosaurus

Archaeopteryx

Procompsognathus

SWITZERLAND

Iguanodon

BELGIUM

Dacentrurus

FRANCE

MONACO

Hypselosaurus

CORSICA (FRANCE)

SARDINIA (ITALY)

Mediterranean Sea

400km

250 miles

0   0

Hylaeosaurus

Lexovisaurus

Atlantic Ocean

Key to European countries:
1 LUXEMBOURG
2 SLOVENIA
3 ANDORRA

Baryonyx

3

SPAIN

Pelicanimimus

Brachiosaurus

PORTUGAL

GIBRALTAR (U.K.)

25

A   B   C   D

4   5   6

DINOSAUR HERD IN BELGIUM

In 1878, a team of Belgian miners found 38 Iguanodon skeletons—the remains of a herd that lived more than 120 million years ago. The dinosaurs might have died when they tried to escape from predators, falling into a deep ravine.

fossilized Iguanodon skeletons

Fossil herd
These skeletons of a Belgian Iguanodon herd are kept together in a museum. It is the largest display of a single type of dinosaur anywhere in the world.

Iguanodon

fossilized dinosaur tracks

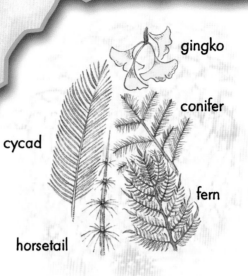

gingko

conifer

cycad

fern

horsetail

Lasting imprint

Like other dinosaurs, Iguanodon often left tracks where it walked in soft mud. Fossilized tracks show that adult Iguanodons usually walked on all fours.

Vegetarian diet

Iguanodon fed only on plants. It ate ferns, horsetails, and many other types of plants, but not grasses—this did not exist when Iguanodon was alive.

27

EUROPEAN DINOSAURS

Most dinosaurs fed on land, but Baryonyx was different. It had jaws like a crocodile's and long claws, especially on its thumbs. It probably waded into the shallows of rivers and lakes and caught fish as they swam past. One fossil of Baryonyx from southern England has fish bones and scales inside it.

Baryonyx

Feeding in the treetops

Brachiosaurus was up to 82 feet (25 meters) long, and its cranelike neck could reach almost twice as high as a giraffe's. It fed on leaves, tearing them off with its peg-shaped teeth. This sauropod lived in Europe, North America, and Africa.

Little grinder

One of the smallest plant-eating dinosaurs, Hypsilophodon had a head the size of an adult human's hand. It fed on low-growing plants, grinding them up with its ridged teeth. It lived in herds and relied on its speed and sharp senses to escape danger, just like deer do today.

fossil of a
Hypsilophodon skull

Chasing lizards

Compsognathus was a small, speedy dinosaur with a chicken-size body and a long neck and tail. It fed on lizards and other small animals, tearing them apart with its claws and teeth.

29

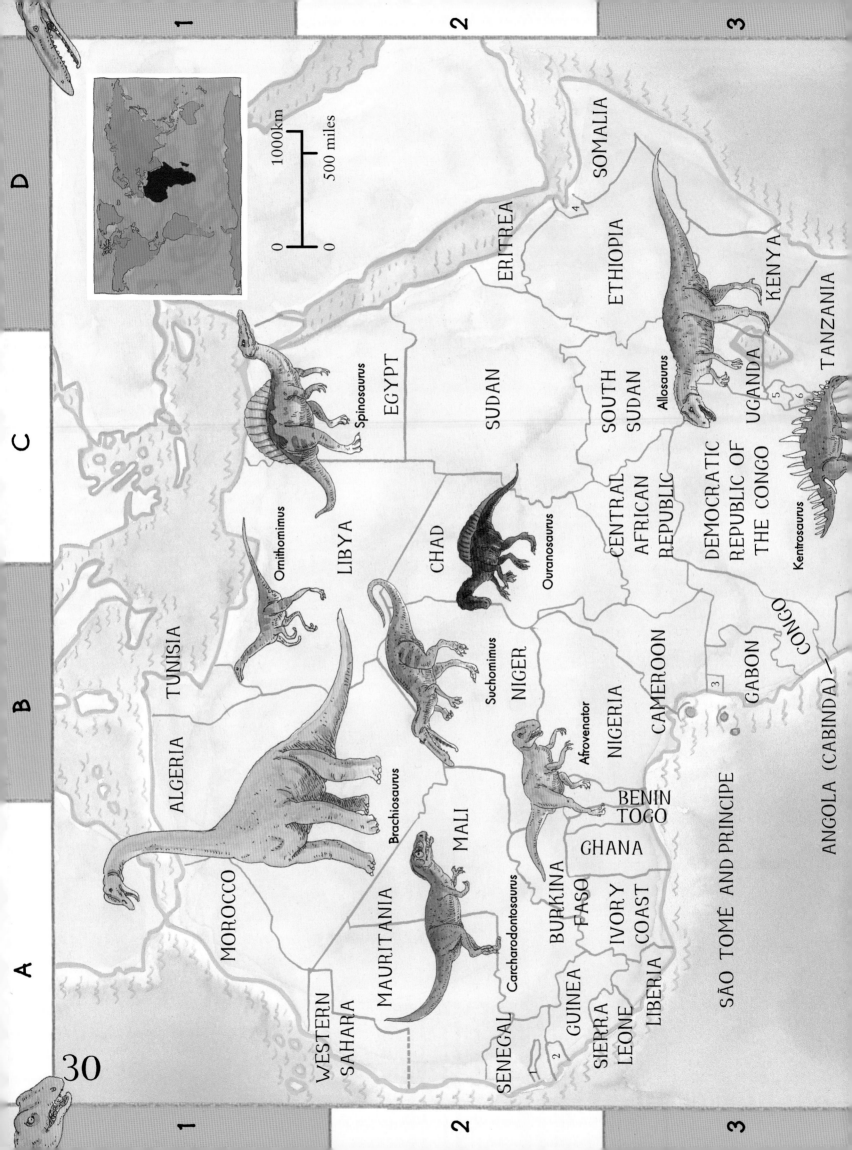

1   2   3

A   B   C   D

1000km
500 miles
0
0

WESTERN SAHARA

MOROCCO

ALGERIA

TUNISIA

LIBYA

EGYPT

Spinosaurus

Ornithomimus

MAURITANIA

MALI

Carcharodontosaurus

SENEGAL

GUINEA

SIERRA LEONE

LIBERIA

IVORY COAST

BURKINA FASO

GHANA

TOGO

BENIN

Afrovenator

NIGER

Suchomimus

CHAD

SUDAN

ERITREA

SOMALIA

ETHIOPIA

SOUTH SUDAN

Allosaurus

KENYA

UGANDA

TANZANIA

Kentrosaurus

DEMOCRATIC REPUBLIC OF THE CONGO

CENTRAL AFRICAN REPUBLIC

Ouranosaurus

NIGERIA

CAMEROON

GABON

CONGO

ANGOLA (CABINDA)

SÃO TOMÉ AND PRINCIPE

Brachiosaurus

COMOROS

4

Ceratosaurus

Majungatholus

MADAGASCAR

Vulcanodon

MOZAMBIQUE

7

Melanorosaurus

Syntarsus

ZAMBIA

8

10

Lesothosaurus

SOUTH AFRICA

11

Heterodontosaurus

ANGOLA

9

Massospondylus

NAMIBIA

Euskelosaurus

Key to African countries:

1   THE GAMBIA
2   GUINEA-BISSAU
3   EQUATORIAL GUINEA
4   DJIBOUTI
5   RWANDA
6   BURUNDI
7   MALAWI
8   ZIMBABWE
9   BOTSWANA
10   ESWATINI
11   LESOTHO

Changing climate

In the Sahara Desert, dinosaur hunters unearth the fossilized remains of Afrovenator, a giant predator discovered in Niger in 1993. When the dinosaur was alive, the Sahara was damp and lush, with plenty of plant-eating prey.

Can you find Afrovenator?

AFRICA

Throughout Africa, dinosaur hunters have found fascinating fossils. They include some of the oldest dinosaurs, as well as the tallest and the most fearsome. Spinosaurus weighed almost twice as much as an African elephant, while Brachiosaurus towered over smaller plant-eating dinosaurs as it browsed the tops of trees.

DUEL IN TANZANIA

In east Africa, a hungry Ceratosaurus tries to attack Kentrosaurus, a slow-moving plant eater. Kentrosaurus is smaller but is protected by bony plates and spikes that are up to 23 inches (58 centimeters) long. Each time the predator moves in, Kentrosaurus swivels around and lashes out with its tail.

Ceratosaurus

Kentrosaurus

Brachiosaurus

Big is best

Brachiosaurus relied on its size to stay out of danger. This enormous plant eater might have weighed up to 80 tons—much more than the biggest predators of its time. But when this giant got old and weak, it was easy prey to a Ceratosaurus.

Ceratosaurus

fossilized skeleton of a Kentrosaurus

Bundle of nerves

Kentrosaurus had a small head and a tiny brain. Above its hips, it had a nerve center, or "second brain," that controlled its back legs and spike-studded tail.

Run for your life

At only 4 feet (1 meter) high, Heterodontosaurus had no hope of fighting Ceratosaurus. Instead, this lightweight dinosaur sprinted away at the first sign of trouble.

Ceratosaurus

Heterodontosaurus

33

AFRICAN DINOSAURS

Spinosaurus was one of the largest predatory dinosaurs, weighing as much as nine tons. In addition to having fearsome teeth and powerful jaws, it had a six-foot- (two-meter-) high "sail." It might have used the sail like a solar panel, soaking up warmth at sunrise and sunset.

Spinosaurus

fossilized skull of a Carcharadontosaurus

Quick exit
Massopondylus lived around 190 million years ago, toward the beginning of the age of dinosaurs. It ate mostly plants and was lightweight. If danger threatened, it sped away on its back legs.

Giant bite
For pure biting power, few dinosaurs could match Carcharadontosaurus. Its skull was 5 feet (1½ meters) long. Its teeth had serrated edges—the biggest teeth were almost as long as a human skull.

Clever hunter
In 1993, researchers found the skeleton of an unknown dinosaur in the Sahara Desert. Although it was 125 million years old, the fossil was almost complete. Called Afrovenator—"African hunter"—it was around 30 feet (9 meters) long. It might have hunted fish in shallow water.

35

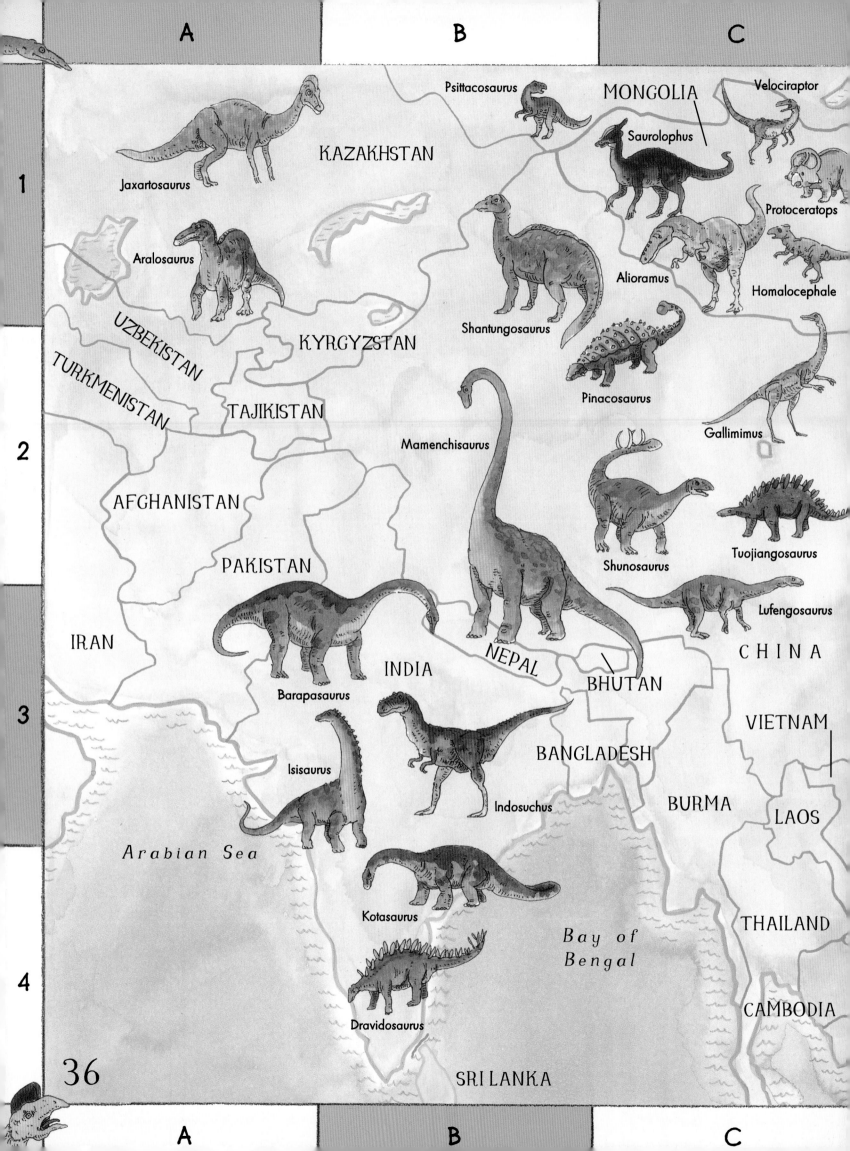

1

Jaxartosaurus

Psittacosaurus

MONGOLIA

Velociraptor

Saurolophus

Protoceratops

Aralosaurus

UZBEKISTAN

TURKMENISTAN

KYRGYZSTAN

Shantungosaurus

Alioramus

Homalocephale

2

TAJIKISTAN

Pinacosaurus

Mamenchisaurus

Gallimimus

AFGHANISTAN

Shunosaurus

Tuojiangosaurus

PAKISTAN

Lufengosaurus

IRAN

Barapasaurus

NEPAL

INDIA

BHUTAN

CHINA

3

Isisaurus

BANGLADESH

VIETNAM

Indosuchus

BURMA

LAOS

Arabian Sea

Kotasaurus

Bay of Bengal

THAILAND

4

CAMBODIA

Dravidosaurus

SRI LANKA

36

RUSSIA

Therizinosaurus

Nemegtosaurus

Microraptor   Sinornithosaurus

Oviraptor   Caudipteryx   Beipiaosaurus

NORTH
KOREA

JAPAN

Tarbosaurus

SOUTH
KOREA   Fukuisaurus   Fukuiraptor

Tsintaosaurus

Pacific Ocean

0 ————————————— 1000km
0 ————————————— 500 miles

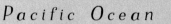

Strong jaws
Protoceratops fossils have been
discovered throughout Mongolia
and China. This fossil shows a
large beak and powerful jaws
that were used to slice and grind
tough leaves and plants.

Can you find
Protoceratops?

ASIA
The dry and windswept deserts of central
Asia have yielded a spectacular amount
of dinosaur fossils. At Mongolia's Flaming
Cliffs, dinosaur hunters have found beaked
plant eaters such as Protoceratops, swift
hunters such as Velociraptor, and amazing
collections of dinosaur eggs. Farther east,
in China, feathered dinosaurs show how
birds evolved.

ASIAN DINOSAURS

Most of today's reptiles don't make any noise, but dinosaurs were very different. Saurolophus, from Asia and North America, made calls by inflating a pouch of skin that was above its snout. These calls would have filled the air when an entire Saurolophus herd spotted danger heading its way.

Large beak
Psittacosaurus, a plant eater, had a beak like a parrot's. It stood just over three feet high at the shoulder but was able to reach taller plants by standing on its back legs.

Tarbosaurus

Saurolophus

arms of a
Deinocheirus fossil

Scary claws

In the late 1960s, researchers
in Mongolia found a huge pair
of arm bones ending in 10-inch
(25-centimeter) long claws. Very
few other bones of their owner,
Deinocheirus, have been found.

Nest raider

Gallimimus fed on the eggs and young
of other dinosaurs, using its arms to
dig and pick up food. Its long neck
helped it spot food that was far away.

DINOSAUR FIGHT IN MONGOLIA

Velociraptor and Protoceratops were deadly enemies. One fossil, found in the Gobi Desert, shows them locked in combat. Velociraptor was attacking with its claws, while Protoceratops hit back with its beak. They died suddenly, probably because they were smothered by a sandstorm or buried by a collapsing dune.

Protoceratops

Velociraptor

fossil of Oviraptor skeleton and eggs

Mother love

Some dinosaurs were very protective parents. This fossil is of an adult Oviraptor that died while sitting on its eggs. Inside each egg there are the tiny bones of the babies.

Low blows

The plant eater Pinacosaurus fought its enemies using a club on the end of its tail. By swinging the club close to the ground, it could smash a predator's legs, knocking it off its feet. Bony armor also helped keep it out of trouble.

Head-to-head collision

Homalocephale had an extra thick layer of bone on the top of its skull. The males might have used this in head-butting contests, fighting to attract mates.

FEATHERED DINOSAURS OF CHINA

In Liaoning, in eastern China, researchers have found dinosaurs with fuzzy outlines of feathers instead of scaly skin. Some—including Caudipteryx—had feathers to stay warm. Others had bigger feathers and used them to fly. Scientists are certain that birds evolved from dinosaurs.

Caudipteryx

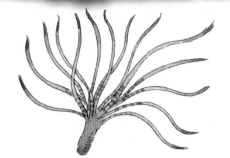

pointed scale   fluffy feather   feather with vanes

From scales to feathers

Feathers evolved gradually from hard, pointed scales. Fluffy feathers evolved first, helping keep dinosaurs warm. From these came much bigger feathers with branched vanes—the type that were inherited by the world's first true birds.

Ground attack

Protarchaeopteryx had long feathers on its arms, but it could not fly. It probably used its feathers like a scoop to catch insects and other small animals.

Winged flier

Microraptor was one of the smallest dinosaurs. It had feathers on its legs and arms, and it probably used all four limbs to fly. Instead of taking off from the ground, it might have jumped from trees.

AUSTRALIA AND NEW ZEALAND

Not many dinosaurs have been found in Australia. This is partly because most of Australia was covered by the ocean for most of the age of dinosaurs. Even so, Australia was the home of unusual dinosaurs, including the giant sauropod Austrosaurus and Minmi, an armored dinosaur covered with bony plates.

Dinosaur trackway

AUSTRALIA

WESTERN AUSTRALIA

Ozraptor

Dino tracks

Australia has some of the best preserved dinosaur trackways. One set, in Western Australia, contains giant footprints that are more than three feet (one meter) wide.

Can you find a trackway?

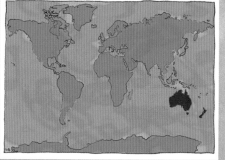

44

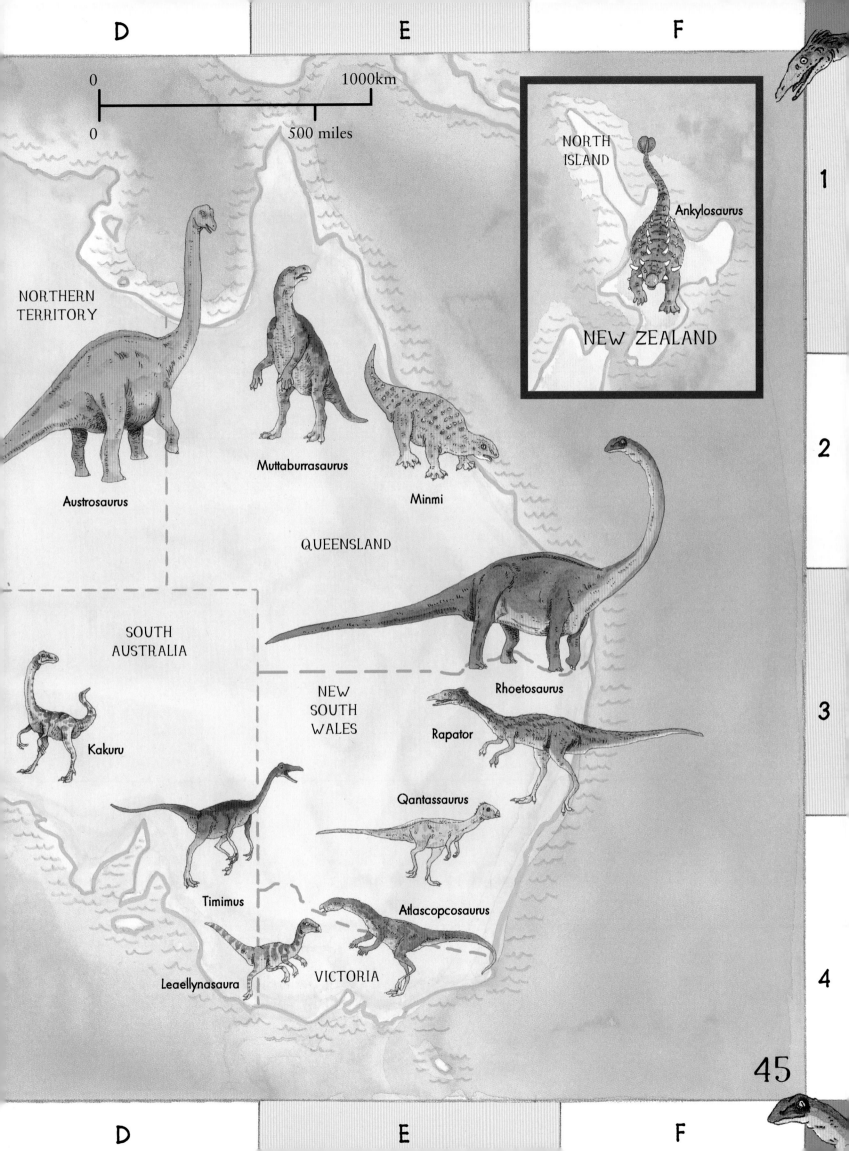

D   E   F

0   1000km
0   500 miles

NORTH
ISLAND

Ankylosaurus

NEW ZEALAND

1

NORTHERN
TERRITORY

Austrosaurus

Muttaburrasaurus

Minmi

2

QUEENSLAND

SOUTH
AUSTRALIA

Rhoetosaurus

Kakuru

NEW
SOUTH
WALES

Rapator

3

Qantassaurus

Timimus

Atlascopcosaurus

Leaellynasaura

VICTORIA

4

45

D   E   F

Glossary

ambush
To attack by surprise.

armored dinosaur
A plant-eating dinosaur protected by tough scales or bony plates.

continent
One of Earth's seven huge areas of land. In the age of dinosaurs, the continents were in different positions than they are today.

crater
A deep hollow made by a volcano or by a meteor hitting Earth.

crest
A large flap on top of a dinosaur's head.

Cretaceous period
The last part of the age of dinosaurs, which ended suddenly when a meteor struck Earth.

dinosaur hunter
Someone who searches for dinosaur fossils and digs them up.

duck-billed dinosaur
A dinosaur with a mouth like a beak and no front teeth. Also known as a hadrosaur.

evolve
To change gradually over thousands or millions of years. As living things evolve, new types gradually appear, while older ones slowly become extinct, or die out.

extinct
No longer living anywhere on Earth. Dinosaurs are now extinct, in addition to many other giant reptiles.

fossil
Hard parts of an animal's body that slowly have changed to stone deep in the ground.

herd
A group of animals that live, feed, and breed together.

horn
A hard body part with a sharp point, usually found on a dinosaur's head.

insect
A small animal with six legs such as a beetle or a bee. The first insects appeared long before the first dinosaurs.

Jurassic period
The middle part of the age of dinosaurs.

limb
A front or back arm or leg.

limestone
A type of layered rock that often contains fossils.

mammal
A warm-blooded animal that feeds its babies milk.

meteor
A piece of rock that has reached Earth from space.

naturalist
Someone who studies animals and plants.

nerves
Parts of the body that work like wiring, helping an animal feel and move.

Pangaea
A huge supercontinent that existed at the beginning of the age of dinosaurs.

predator
An animal that hunts other animals for its food.

prehistoric
Anything that lived in the distant past, long before human history began.

prey
An animal that is hunted and eaten by other animals.

quarry
A place where rock is dug up so that it can be used. Quarries are often good places for finding fossils.

reptile
A cold-blooded animal with scaly skin that usually breeds by laying eggs. Dinosaurs were the biggest reptiles that ever lived.

sauropod
A huge, long-necked dinosaur that fed on plants. The largest dinosaurs were all sauropods.

scales
Small, hard plates that cover a reptile's skin.

scavenging
Feeding on the remains of dead animals.

serrated
Having jagged edges.

trackway
A place where dinosaurs often walked, leaving fossilized footprints.

Triassic period
The first part of the age of dinosaurs.

46

Index

Each dinosaur name has a pronunciation guide in parentheses after its entry.

47

Photographic acknowledgments

The Publisher would like to thank the following for permission to reproduce their material. Every care has been taken to trace copyright holders. However, if there have been unintentional omissions or failure to trace copyright holders, we apologize and will, if informed, endeavor to make corrections in any future edition.

Pages: 5 Natural History Museum, London/Science Photo Library; 9 Wolfgang Kaehler/LightRocket via Getty; 13 Jim Amos/Science Photo Library; 15 Martin Leber/Shutterstock; 19 D. van Ravenswaay/Science Photo Library; 20 MAF/Alamy; 22 Dr Andrew Cuff; 24 Akkharat Jarusilawong/Shutterstock; 26 picturelibrary/Alamy; 27 University Corporation for Atmospheric Research/Science Photo Library; 29 Natural History Museum; 31 Didier Dutheil/Sygma via Getty Images; 33 Faviel_Raven/Shutterstock; 35 Arco Images GmbH/Alamy; 37 Natural History Museum; 39 Natural History Museum; 41 Louie Psihoyos/Corbis; 44 katclay/iStock